WEALTH BUILDING
SECRETS FROM THE BIBLE

*The Believer's Journey to a Faithful,
Generous, and Financially Free Life*

PASTOR JONATHAN GERACI

To my parents,

who taught me the secrets of wealth building at an early age.

TABLE OF CONTENTS

Chapter 1: Biblical Wealth   **1**

The Realization   3

Biblical Financial Habits   5

Steve's Transformation with Proverbs   6

The Challenge   8

Chapter 2: Why Be Wealthy?   **11**

The Argument   13

A Responsibility   14

A Joy in Stewardship   15

Work Ethic   18

Legacy   19

The Fruit of The Spirit   21

Testimony   26

Biblical Examples of Wealthy People   27

Modern Examples   30

Summary   32

Chapter 3: Money Myths   35

It's Evil!   37

Jealousy   39

Fear of Losing   41

Fear of Missing Out   44

Fear of the Last Days   45

Identify Your Fears   47

The Challenge   49

Chapter 4: Secret #1 – Contentment   51

Esau's Example   53

The Comparing Game   55

The "Thneed"   58

Ask Yourself, Why?   60

What Brings You Joy?   61

Sell All That Has You   64

Budgeting   67

Financial Freedom   74

The Challenge   78

Chapter 5: Secret #2 – Freedom from Debt   81

Debt Is an Emergency   83

Emotional Consequences   87

Spiritual Consequences 88

The Good Debt Myth 90

The Change 95

Debt Snowball 98

The Challenge 101

Chapter 6: Secret #3 – Faithfulness **103**

Winter Is Coming 105

Diligence 106

Work Ethic 109

Building the School of the Prophets 111

Faithfulness in Savings 114

Four Strategies for Investing 118

Betty's Story 124

Chapter 7: Secret #4 – Generosity **127**

Give away the Best 129

Gaining Wealth by Giving 129

Do Not Trust in Riches 130

The World Gives to Givers 132

All That Is Not Given away Is Lost 135

Chapter 8: The Launching Pad   **137**

Appendix   **145**

About the Author   147

Acknowledgments   149

Fear-Setting Worksheet   151

The Seven Tips To Attend College Debt-Free   153

DOWNLOAD THE AUDIOBOOK FOR FREE!

Thank you for taking the time to invest in your future. It is the best investment that you can make.

Thank you for applying God's Word into your everyday life.

If you would like the free audiobook, please visit www.wealthbuildingsecrets.net/audio-book

CHAPTER 1

BIBLICAL WEALTH

THE REALIZATION

Emma was crying. Tears were streaming down her face. There were pages of numbers in front of her and the numbers meant something. She was in trouble.

Emma and her husband were Christians.

They knew their Bibles but failed to apply Biblical principles to their money.

This affected every other area of their lives.

We sat down and started looking at their financial reality. That started the tears—they realized that they were spending $4,000 a month even though they were only making $1,000 a month. And they acknowledged that they were in trouble. For the first time in their lives, they realized that they were drowning financially.

Emma and Ethan have a major problem. A problem that is the #1 leading cause of divorce—money. The average rate of divorce in America is 50%.[1] Unfortunately, among Christians, the percentage is not much better. However, Tom Corley did a study among wealthy individuals, and the divorce rate is only 20%.[2] Why so low?

What habits do the wealthy have that mimic simple Biblical principles?

I shared with Emma and Ethan my own journey. How my wife and I lived well below the poverty line before we learned to practice a few simple money habits. I offered to share a few Biblical secrets for getting their finances in order. Also, if she was interested, I suggested that Emma could go shopping with my wife and she could see firsthand how my wife spent only a fourth of what Emma was spending on groceries.

As a pastor, I have had many people like Emma and Ethan call for financial assistance. In each instance, the caller

[1] http://www.apa.org/topics/divorce/

[2] http://richhabits.net/marry-well-if-you-want-to-be-happy-healthy-and-wealthy/ retrieved October 25, 2017

presents an emergency situation that he or she is desperate to get out of. When those emergencies began to occur on a regular basis, I realized that I have not been providing long-term solutions.

BIBLICAL FINANCIAL HABITS

In multiple places, the Bible lays out the principles of building wealth. Proverbs 14:24 tells us, "The crown of the wise is their riches, but the foolishness of fools is folly."

When we apply God's word in our daily lives, we will live more abundantly.[3] These are universal principles—and also Christian principles.

This pathway to financial freedom takes sacrifice.

If you are looking for a prosperity gospel, please stop reading and throw this book in the trash. While I believe in God's blessing,

---

[3] John 10:10

> **I am always amazed when people expect God's blessing when they are not following God's counsel.**

It's kind of like me telling my two-year-old son that the stove is hot and not to touch it. When I turn my back, my son goes over and touches the stove. I warned him, he didn't listen, and he faced the consequences of his actions.

The Bible explains key habits to change your financial future for the better, but you must take that information and use it to review and modify your habits. Modern researchers have confirmed these principles. What do you know? God knew what He was talking about!

STEVE'S TRANSFORMATION WITH PROVERBS

Steve was depressed. Since graduating from college, he had failed in every job he'd had. It didn't matter what he did, he couldn't make his bosses happy. He felt like a failure. One day, he shared his woes with a close friend, who replied, "Do you want to be smarter than all your bosses?"

"Yeah, right!" Steve responded.

His friend continued, "I bet you could be a millionaire within five years!"

That certainly caught Steve's attention. He was curious now.

His friend and mentor responded: "I want you to read through the book of Proverbs, one chapter a day. Get a journal and start writing down the lessons that you learn."

Steve took his friend's advice, following the path of many great men in history. George Washington, Thomas Jefferson, Abraham Lincoln, Henry Ford, and Thomas Edison were all readers of Proverbs.

In less than two years, Steve was applying those principles in a marketing start-up company. A few months later, he was making a million dollars a week.[4] The book of Proverbs changed Steve's life. Will you allow it to change yours?

---

[4] Scott, Steven K. "The Richest Man Who Ever Lived". Random House Press. 2006

THE CHALLENGE

I never heard from Emma and Ethan again. Their bank accounts were hemorrhaging, but they seemed to be comfortable with that. It was easier for them to call for a handout than to change their habits and follow Biblical wisdom.

How about you? Are you willing to make a Biblical change in your habits that could stabilize and increase your wealth?

God has promised to give each of us the fruit of the Spirit, and when I follow those principles in my everyday life God will bless me.

When I show kindness to my wife, my relationship prospers. When I show self-control in my diet, my health improves. When I exhibit gentleness, or a willingness to yield, the Holy Spirit can lead me to new truth. And when I show faithfulness in finances and keep investing month after month, I will be able to live my retirement dreams. Christian growth is not limited to growth in our spiritual lives, but in all areas—mental, physical, social, spiritual, and financial.

The principles in this book are taken from scripture, but they are universal principles that, if applied, will affect everyone and everything you come in contact with.

God gives a warning to the church of Laodicea, the last-day church, "So then, because you are lukewarm, and neither cold nor hot, I will vomit you out of My mouth."[5] That translates to:

"You need to make a choice. Quit sitting on the fence."

Every day a good faithful Jew would recite, "You shall love the Lord your God, with all your heart, with all your soul, and with all your strength."[6] This is total commitment. Are you willing to go all the way with God?

God wants you to be the head and not the tail, and He has given principles that will lead you to be "healthy, wealthy, and wise".[7] [8] He gives you blessings so that you will be a

---

[5] Revelation 3:16

[6] Deuteronomy 6:5, 6

[7] Deuteronomy 28

[8] attributed to Benjamin Franklin

9

blessing to other people and point people to Christ. Matthew reminds us, "Let your light so shine before men, that they may see your good works and glorify your Father in heaven."[9]

In His Word, God has blessed us with the wisdom and habits that will also be a blessing to other people. Will you search for these principles? Will you join me in this journey, investigating how a 2,700-year-old book is still relevant in the area of personal finance?[10]

We are going to start with a question. "Why Be Wealthy?

---

[9] Matthew 5:16

[10] http://bigthink.com/paul-ratner/how-old-is-the-bible retrieved October 25, 2017

CHAPTER 2

WHY BE WEALTHY?

THE ARGUMENT

"Get the phone."

"No, you get the phone."

Neither Jim nor Barbara would get the phone because both knew who would probably be calling. Bill collectors. Not just one, but countless bill collectors.

Their marriage had become one series of arguments after another about the same thing—money, or more appropriately, the lack of it.

Was this God's ideal?

Did God really intend marriage to be filled with one argument after the other?

If the fruit of the Spirit is peace, why are we "not feeling it"?

When you follow God's plan for your finances, you will be amazed by how God blesses you. There are simple Biblical principles for the way God wants you to handle His money.

13

A RESPONSIBILITY

A steward is someone who watches over and takes care of a resource for someone else. God has called us to be stewards of the finances He has given us.

Imagine that you were employed as the financial manager for Acme Corporation, and you could only use the same financial practices that you use in your own home. Would you be fired from your position? If you practiced the same policies in your professional life that you do in your personal life, what would be the result? If God audited your personal finances, what would He find?

"It's not a big deal that I have debt, I can still spoil myself."

"I deserve to go out for coffee. You wouldn't believe the stress I'm under."

We constantly make excuses for indulging our desires. We forget that our money is not really *our* money but *God's* money.

If God audited our personal finances—which are really His finances—what would He find?

In Matthew 25:14-30, Christ told the parable of a master who gave three of his servants different talents before he left on a journey. Each servant used the funds in a different way. The first didn't do anything but bury it. The second, who received two talents, invested them and received two more. The one who received five talents doubled his as well. Sometimes, we spiritualize this parable and say the talents are the gifts God has given us, and that is a reasonable application. But Christ was talking about money. How we deal with our personal finances is a window to what is in our hearts.

A JOY IN STEWARDSHIP

"As for every man to whom God has given riches and wealth, and given him power to eat of it, to receive his heritage and rejoice in his labour—this *is* the gift of God. For he will not dwell unduly on the days of his life, because God keeps *him* busy with the joy of his heart." (Ecclesiastes 5:19-20).

Wealth is a gift from God. Whether I have a lot or a little, I am only here to manage what God has given me.

If I am only the manager, then I should consult the owner about how He wants me to manage His possessions. We are God's stewards for the purpose of Him bringing us personal joy.

"Command those who are rich in this present age not to be haughty, nor to trust in uncertain riches but in the living God, who gives us richly all things to enjoy. Let them do good, that they be rich in good works, ready to give, willing to share." (1 Timothy 6:17-18).

It is easy to focus on the gift than it is to focus on the giver of the gift.

God gives us wealth so that we can be a blessing to other people, and that brings us joy.

"It is more blessed to give than receive." (Acts 20:35).

16

"Therefore, if you have not been faithful in the unrighteous mammon, who will commit to your trust the true riches?" (Luke 16:11).

If we cannot wisely handle the small amount that God gives us, why would He give us more? And if we can't handle earthly riches appropriately, how will we handle heavenly ones? Money is a test to see how we handle what God has given us.

Managing your money is a sign of commitment to God. ★

In the Bible, the first reference to a tithe was as a sign of commitment between Abraham and God. In Genesis 14:20, it is a sign of worship.

Malachi went as far as to say, "Will a man rob God? Yet ye have robbed Me. But you say, 'Wherein have we robbed you?' In tithes and offerings." (Malachi 3:8). Good stewardship is the responsibility of every follower of God. Christ said, "For where your treasure is, there your heart will be also." (Matthew 6:21). Where have you stored the treasure that God has given you?

God has asked you and me to manage His resources. How we handle those resources shows our priorities and commitment to Him.

WORK ETHIC

"Whatever your hand finds to do, do it with all your might." (Ecclesiastes 9:10). God is calling us to have a good work ethic.

> # When we focus on working for the Lord, and not for a human employer, people will notice.

Rabbi Lapin comments, "If you do a good job, people will reward you with certificates of appreciation called dollar bills."[11] The more excellent the job, the more you will be rewarded for your effort.

Ecclesiastes 5:18 says that when we focus on the work God has called us to do, we will experience joy. When we are

---

[11] Lapin, Daniel, "Thou Shall Prosper", Wiley Publishing. 2009.

passionate about what we are doing, we will do it with excellence and will be rewarded both on this earth and in heaven.

Tom Corley says, "Passion trumps intelligence, so pursue your passion."[12]

When you look at the habits of wealthy individuals, you will discover that they are Christian character habits.

LEGACY

God wants you to be wealthy so that you will leave a legacy. "A good person leaves an inheritance for their children's children, but a sinner's wealth is stored up for the righteous."[13] That kind of legacy only happens because of intentional, long-term planning. It happens because you have a vision for where you want to be in 30 years. This is much like the vision that Moses had when he chose to

---

[12] Corley, Tom, "Change Your Habits, Change Your Life", North Loop Books. 2016.

[13] Proverbs 13:22 NIV

forsake pleasure for a time because he had a greater reward in mind.[14]

Leaving a legacy is not only about leaving money to your grandchildren, but leaving them with the knowledge to handle the money without ruining their lives. Money is a good servant, but a poor master.

Many years ago, there was a family who saw a need for domestic steel production. This family excelled at what they did, and people were happy to acknowledge that fact by giving them money. The family enjoyed the money, but they also made sure that they set up something that left blessings for the generations to come. Andrew Carnegie saw that living a good life was not just about himself. He had a plan for the future. His donations to libraries, education, and more totalled over $350 million.[15]

Christ came to give you freedom, to give you life, and to help you live more abundantly.

---

[14] Hebrews 11:24, 25

[15] https://www.thefamouspeople.com/profiles/andrew-carnegie-217.php. retrieved October 20, 2017

> ## You cannot experience the freedom Christ has for you while you are suffocating in debt.

What would financial freedom look like for you? It means you can take an internship that doesn't pay well but will give you more life experience. Financial freedom means that you can serve the Lord as a missionary without worrying about how little, if anything, you will be paid.

Right out of college, I served as a missionary. I wasn't paid a lot; many times, I wondered if I would be paid at all that month. I had learned the wealth-building secrets from the Bible and, while it was annoying not to get paid on time, I had peace because I knew I had an emergency fund. Why does God want you to be wealthy? Because we can rightly reflect Him when we have financial freedom.

THE FRUIT OF THE SPIRIT

I had just finished a nine-part sermon series on the Fruit of the Spirit. "But the fruit of the Spirit is love, joy, peace, longsuffering, kindness, goodness, faithfulness, gentleness,

21

self-control. Against such, there is no law." (Galatians 5:22, 23).

While reading a financial book, I thought about those past nine weeks and noticed how many fruits of the Spirit, when applied to our financial lives, would help us to build wealth.

The fruit of the Spirit is *love*—and Christ said, "Perfect love casts out fear." (1 John 4:18). Do I have that perfect love for God and love for my fellow man that calls me to manage my finances? This will motivate me to think about how I spend the Lord's money. If I act out of love, and not out of fear, it will provide a sense of freedom.

The fruit of the Spirit is *joy*. Joy is something that motivates and endures when things are good or when trials come into our lives. It's the joy of seeing a goal fulfilled when we have the self-control to give up short-term pleasures for long-term goals.

"Looking unto Jesus, the author and finisher of our faith, who for the joy that was set before him, He endured the cross." (Hebrews 12:2). Christ took short-term pains to experience long-term pleasure. The joy of spending eternity with you and me is what drove Christ to the cross. If you consider the joy of financial freedom, what would it look like to you? Maybe it's being able to pay for your kids' college education? Maybe it's saving for retirement. What is the joy you want to experience in financial freedom? Maybe it is the joy of giving to other people—which is the most incredible joy that I have ever experienced. And doing it anonymously will increase the spiritual rewards.

The fruit of the Spirit is *peace*. When I have peace in my life, I have contentment, which is the desired harmony between God and man. I don't need the newest or neatest or "Thneed". Thank you, Dr. Seuss, for that word. Thneed means something that I think that I need. When I have God's peace in my life, it allows me to say, "I have enough".

The fruit of the Spirit is *longsuffering*; some Bible translations say patience. In my pursuit of financial freedom, I have a savings account. I will wait on God's timing if I don't have the money for what I need. I am not infatuated with the newest get-rich-quick scheme because I have patience while I wait for God to let me know the time is right.

The fruit of the Spirit is *kindness*. This can be described as usefulness. When I have an emergency fund, it is useful (kind) to my family. They will feel peace instead of stress when the car breaks down. They will not panic when a major household appliance quits because they know that they have the resources to replace it. Showing kindness is being useful to my family and planning ahead for retirement so I do not spend my last days as a burden to my children.

The fruit of the Spirit is *goodness*. This can be defined as an attitude of generosity; it is going the extra mile. Some commentaries say generosity is "profitable kindness." Generosity is a habit of wealthy people, and poor people will say they don't have enough to share. Being generous increases the joy and peace in my life.

The fruit of the spirit is *faithfulness*—a strong sense of duty. The Old Testament likens faithfulness to the physical pillars that hold up a building. When I show faithfulness in my finances, I will maintain diligence in my investing strategy, day in or day out. Financial analysts call this "dollar cost averaging", which we will see is a biblical principle. I don't have to worry because I will faithfully invest. I will not be caught with fear because I have God's peace.

The fruit of the spirit is *gentleness*—gentleness reveals itself in a willingness to yield, reminiscent of a lamb being lead to slaughter. When I am self-sacrificing in my finances, I work longer hours to get out of debt. I realize that the crazy work schedule is not forever. I am striving for financial freedom that will be a monetary blessing to my family—and it will also be a spiritual blessing to my family. When I sacrifice my want of the newest iPhone because I want to set up my children's college fund, I am practicing gentleness—a willingness to yield to a greater vision than my own temporal desires.

The fruit of the Spirit is *self-control*. What would happen if I practiced self-control in my finances? "I would tell my money where to go, instead of at the end of the month wondering where it went."[16] I would create a budget, for that means demonstrating self-control with my money.

"Discipline equals freedom."[17] The more disciplined I am with my finances, the more I can give and the more

---

[16] Attributed to Michael Hyatt

[17] Quote by Jocko Willick, former Navy SEAL, personal trainer/coach

freedom I will discover in my life. When I can do that over the long term, it is called early retirement.

The fruits of the Spirit can be found in every aspect of life—physical, mental, social, financial, and spiritual. The fruits of the Spirit are a gift from God. As Christians, can we have the fruit of the Spirit in one area of our lives without it being manifested in every area? When we struggle with self-control in our finances, when we struggle with patience in how we handle money, we need to pray that God will give us the fruits of the Spirit and the power to overcome.

TESTIMONY

I don't make a lot of money as a pastor. In fact, many people would consider my family close to the poverty line. But my wife and I have learned habits of wealth building from the Bible. We have learned to enjoy the simple things in life. And if we are faithful to this Biblical journey, our financial picture will look a lot different in 20 years. We practice these wealth-building secrets and, as a result, my wife has the freedom to be a stay-at-home mom while the kids are still young. It has allowed us to make choices based on what is important to us.

My wife and I spent our first year of marriage living in an RV year-round, making $12,000 between the two of us. It was hard at times, but it was also rewarding to see how God provided, even when unexpected medical expenses came up.

God is faithful. Biblical wealth-building secrets are effective for any income bracket, and they will work when you put them to work.

BIBLICAL EXAMPLES OF WEALTHY PEOPLE

The Bible is full of stories about wealthy people who used their riches to be a blessing to other people. One of the oldest books in the Bible, the book of Job, documents the life of a wealthy man who lost everything. Even his closest friends turned against him. Yet he remained faithful to God. Job was not defined by his possessions, and his sufferings and trials were a witness to those around him.

Abraham of the Old Testament was a wealthy man with many flocks. As an offering to God, he gave his first fruits, the first of what he had been given. This is the first time in the Bible that tithe is mentioned—returning 10% of your income to God. By giving tithe, Abraham acknowledged God as the central aspect of his life. He had a generous spirit, which is one of the keys to building wealth. In his book, "Give and Grow Rich", Omen Redden notes that one of the qualities of wealthy individuals is that they are generous.

Solomon was the wealthiest man in the entire world. His yearly salary was $960 million in today's dollars.[18] Solomon didn't start his life as a king with a search for wealth. 1 Kings 3 says that God asked Solomon what he would like. With a humble spirit, Solomon replied with his request for wisdom—the wisdom to be able to discern right from wrong. God replied, "Not only will I give you wisdom, but also I will give you riches, honour, and fame." In response, people from all known parts of the world came to Israel to

---

[18] https://www.quora.com/What-is-the-estimate-of-king-solomons-wealth-in-todays-economy-and-is-he-the-likely-richest retrieved October 22, 2017. Modified numbers for gold being $1,200 per ounce today.

learn what made the God of Heaven—Solomon's God—different.

Throughout the Old Testament, we see a curious evangelistic strategy. In Deuteronomy 28, God tells Israel, "If you follow Him, He will make you the head and not the tail. He will bless you so that you may be a blessing to other people." The Old Testament model of evangelism is that God blesses Israel and other nations notice, go to Israel, and ask questions because everyone wants to be a part of what is happening.

The Old Testament rarely mentions God sending missionaries to other lands—Jonah may be one of the few examples. The missionary strategy seems simple: God blessed His people, others noticed, and they asked for an explanation. Then, they also wanted to serve the God of heaven.

In the New Testament, God's evangelistic strategy changed "Go ye therefore, and teach all nations . . ." (Matthew 28:19), and missionaries were sent to the ends of the earth.

The New Testament mentions a wealthy person who was influential in furthering the gospel work.

Nicodemus not only used his influence as a Jew in a high position to be a blessing to Jesus's ministry, but he went full force into the gospel ministry after Christ's death and accession. He financially supported the spreading of the gospel unto the ends of the world.

MODERN EXAMPLES

Most wealthy individuals are not as flashy as those displayed in the Hollywood tabloids. Instead, they faithfully and quietly go about following wealth-building habits. In the book "The Millionaire Next Door", Thomas J. Stanley mentions that most millionaires don't drive new vehicles, but reliable used vehicles. They are not about trying to impress people with their wealth.

When Garwin McNeilus began working in the construction business in the 1960s, he learned that it was difficult to get concrete to the worksite. What did he come up with? A more reliable cement truck. Now, years later, about a third of the cement trucks that are on the road today have his family name on their trucks. Today, the McNeilus family is very generous in supporting humanitarian and missionary work in undeveloped areas. They have been blessed and, in return, they are a blessing to other people.[19]

Tim didn't start off with a lot. In fact, he worked in a missionary position for the first 7 years of his married life. He then got into the farming business and developed a large workforce in the Midwest. The first time I met him, he was passing out Christian literature and he gave me a stack of DVD sermons. He was a businessman with the heart of a pastor.

God calls each one into ministry—into sharing himself with other people. Sometimes, that is in a position as a pastor. Other times, that is as a businessman, farmer, cook, or homemaker. Tim's generosity and his enthusiasm for ministry were contagious to everyone he met. When his children grew up, they followed his example to be a blessing to those in their community. Whether he had a lot or a little, Tim was always a generous man who was committed to the Lord's work.

---

[19] https://www.mcneiluscompanies.com/about/company-history/
https://vimeo.com/53420712 retrieved October 22, 2017

Wealth didn't change the character of these people, as some believe. It only revealed even more of the people who they really were inside.

The Bill and Melinda Gates Foundation uses its money to be a blessing to others and to solve large problems in the world.[20] One of its goals is to eradicate polio, which is a debilitating disease that affects children in many parts of the world. The Gates Foundation is solving problems that no one else is taking on.

SUMMARY

God gives wealth so that we can be a blessing to other people. Managing God's money His way will bring us joy and a sense of purpose. When we apply the fruits of the Spirit in our financial lives, we will build wealth. A work ethic is merely realizing that we work for the Lord and not

---

[20] This is one family I don't know personally.

for man. When we build wealth, we will have an opportunity to leave a family legacy to future generations.

Wealth is not a number or goal. It is God's resource and we must use it His way. Wealth is God's plan.

CHAPTER 3

MONEY MYTHS

IT'S EVIL!

Whenever you attempt to do something good, there will be people trying to distract you. In the early Christian church after Christ went back to heaven and the early disciples were trying to organize a movement, the group became distracted. They strayed from the teachings of Jesus and became heretics.

Financial writer Dave Ramsey describes this group of people in his book "The Legacy Journey". The Gnostics went against the Bible and one of the false doctrines they preached was that all physical things, including material possessions, were evil. This group believed that all possessions and money were inherently evil. 2,000 years later, you can still see the same heresy. Their theory is that if you have a nice house or a nice car, you must not be spiritual.

1 Timothy 6:10 says "For the love of money is a root of all kinds of evil." It doesn't say that all money is evil. God wants us to worship Him, and Him alone. He wants us to "love the Lord our God with all our heart, and with all of

our soul, and with all of our mind."[21] Anything that gets in the way of that is idolatry. That could be relationships, it could be a career, it could be hobbies, it could even be our money. What is Satan is trying to distract you with?

According to Francis Bacon, "Money makes a good servant, but a bad master." I know rich people who are distracted by their money, and it takes them away from their walk with God. I know not-so-rich people, even pastors, who are distracted by their struggles with managing money. And it always affects their walk with God.

The media loves to tell us that all rich people are the same. This "all or nothing" mentality is a psychological distortion. All rich people are jerks. Have you met rich people who are jerks? I have. Have you met poor people who are jerks? I have as well. Money seems to reflect the character that is already there.

In his book "Give and Grow Rich", Omer Redden comments that

---

[21] Deuteronomy 6:5, 6

> **"God doesn't hate rich people; He hates greed, pride, and selfishness in people."**

At the end of every radio show, Dave Ramsey says, "There is only one way to financial peace and that is to walk daily with the Prince of Peace, Christ Jesus."

Will you walk daily with him? Do you want to dedicate every area of your life to him, including your finances?

JEALOUSY

> **People love to be jealous of what others have, but they usually don't covet the work that it took to get to that place.**

And what might be an 18-year process of sweat, blood, and tears to reach that wealthy status is too-often reported by the media as an "overnight success".

It's easy to be jealous of those overnight successes. "The Accidental Billionaires" tells the story of Mark Zuckerberg and his focus on creating Facemash, which eventually developed into Facebook. Zuckerberg forfeited sleep, parties, and a social life because of his focus.

Why are people jealous of wealthy people? Because it provides an excuse to be lazy and not take personal responsibility. It's easier to cast the blame on the government or on other people—then I give myself permission to be jealous because it's not *my* fault. I don't have to wake up early or stay up late or focus on changing my financial situation.

Success comes when I take personal responsibility for my actions.

Taking personal responsibility is uncomfortable. It's always easier to blame someone else. But I've learned that if you follow these simple Biblical principles, this wealth-building wisdom can change your financial destiny.

Pastor Phil Smith served in Washington as a pastor. He traveled internationally, speaking about Christian principles on money. During his lifetime, he spent thousands of dollars on self-education and attending financial seminars. His ministry blessed many people, but he still had the attitude of "Don't get wealthy, because wealthy people are evil." It's always easier to villainize someone rather than to ask how they got where they are. While Smith presented many programs about money, his personal financial situation did not look good. He was not practicing the Biblical principles of wealth building.

FEAR OF LOSING

There once were three servants, each given different amounts of money. In His parable of the talents, Christ instructed each servant to be responsible and multiply what he had been given. But the one who was given the least was afraid of losing it, so he buried his money. Then, the master returned and asked for an accounting of what he had left to each servant. He was most severe on the person who buried his money instead of trying to multiply it.

Proverbs 22:13 says,

> **"The lazy man says, 'There is a lion outside! I shall be slain in the streets!'"**

So, that man never goes outside for fear the lion will get him. Some people don't invest in the stock market because they fear losing everything. In "The Truth about Money", Ric Edelman describes the stock market as a boy playing with a yo-yo—the yo-yo goes up, the yo-yo goes down. But this boy playing with his toy is also going uphill. If you focus on the yo-yo, it's easy to be terrified, but if you focus on the uphill path, it will not seem so scary.

The stock market is like that. If you focus on the daily gains and losses, you might have to up your heart medication. But if you invest wisely, then step back and look at the 5-year and 10-year track record, you will sleep better at night.

Seneca the Younger was a Roman philosopher who spent several days a month in voluntary poverty. He wore old ratty clothes, ate the scantest fare, and then asked himself, "Is this the thing I fear so much?" Often our fears are not based on reality but on our gross exaggeration of our reality. Fear is a debilitating thing. Fear will keep us safe, but it can also prevent us from accomplishing what God has called us to accomplish in life.

We may fear having too many options. In his book, "The Paradox of Choice," Barry Schwartz says that the more options we have, the less satisfied we will be with the option we choose, and the more likely that we will become overwhelmed and not choose any option.

When it comes to finances, we have a huge number of choices: Should I buy that new pair of jeans that look so good on me? Should I save for my kids' education? When it comes to investing, it is mental overload: should I go with mutual funds? Stocks? Private equity? Bitcoin? With too many choices, it's easy to get overwhelmed, stall out, and do nothing. When we get to the savings chapter, we will talk about investment strategies that will keep you from feeling overwhelmed.

FEAR OF MISSING OUT

"Have you seen what Bitcoin is doing?" Sam tried to convince me why I needed to buy it.

"It has been going up a crazy amount. The past few months it has risen 796% You have to do this! This is a game changer!"

Everyone wants to be where the action is. Everyone wants to make a quick buck, but Proverbs 28:22 tells us that the quickest way to poverty is trying to get rich quick. Warren Buffet says, "You need to be fearful when other people are greedy, and greedy when other people are fearful." It pretty much follows the sage investing advice, "Buy low and sell high."

Bitcoin is the current rage, as of this writing. A decade ago, it was the dot-com boom. In the 1600s it was tulips. There will always be some hot stock pick that everyone is recommending. I have had friends who have made money in crypto-currency. I also have friends who have lost a lot of money on their investments in crypto-currency.

It is so easy to get caught up with FOMO, the Fear of Missing Out. When we apply FOMO to our finances, we will lose money. We need to do careful research on what we invest in rather than make decisions based on emotions.

FEAR OF THE LAST DAYS

Some Christians look at world events and recognize that we are living in the last days. It is tempting to ask, "Why should I worry about my personal finances if Christ is going to come back so soon?" If you listen to the news, it seems that every report about the stock market is gloom and doom. Yes, we are facing the end of the world. But it has not happened yet.

Why do we hear so much about the housing market crash, the stock market crash, the economic crash, and every other crash? Simple. Because fear sells. The news media is just trying to sell their products and avoid their own crashes.

Wikipedia documents 20 stock market crashes since the great Wall Street crash of 1929. I do believe that the Bible teaches that the world will end. I believe that Matthew 24 and the books of Daniel and Revelation give us warnings of current and coming events. I also believe that there will be financial turmoil at the end of time— see James 5 and Revelation 18.

The Saving the Crumbs blog, Alistair Huong, gives three reasons for not using the stock market to predict the end of the world.[22] Number one, forecasting the movement of the stock market is foolish. Even Warren Buffet admits that he doesn't know where the stock market will go in the short term. Number two, forecasting which crash will be the last is doubly impossible. There have been so many crashes in the past, how will we know which one will be the largest and final crash? Third, the Bible tells us to stop trying. Matthew 24:36 says, "No man knows the day or the hour."

Christ tells us to occupy till He comes. That means we shouldn't build bunkers and prepare for the apocalypse. We need to wisely realize the time, but remember that realizing the time has more to do with caring about the salvation of our friends and neighbours.

---

[22] http://www.savingthecrumbs.com/2016/03/stock-market-end-of-the-world/, retrieved on October 22, 2017

IDENTIFY YOUR FEARS

"You should define your fears instead of your goals." That advice is from Tim Ferriss in his eponymous TED Talk. Every month, Tim Ferriss does a fear-setting exercise instead of goal-setting.

Seneca says,

> **"We suffer more often in imagination than in reality."**

Fear-setting is visualizing the worst-case scenario and what you would do to mitigate it when that happens. It is separating yourself from what you can control and what you can't. It is really about having self-control, another fruit of the Spirit.

Here is a simple guide to fear-setting. Take out three pieces of paper. First, ask yourself: What do I fear? Is it asking someone out? Quitting my job? Asking for a promotion or a raise? Taking a vacation? Then define the worst case possible—write down 10 to 20 things about this question that make you afraid. For example, taking a vacation. One fear might be that it would rain, and you would be depressed throughout your trip; another fear might be that you would miss an important letter, say from the IRS, and they would shut down your business.

Title your next column "Prevent". List all the things you can do to prevent those awful things that you imagine might happen. Let's go back to the fear of a rainy vacation, and your possible depression. You might repair the damage by getting a blue light to help with depression. To prevent missing an important IRS letter, you could arrange to forward your business mail to your accountant so that nothing would be ignored.

The third column is "Repair". If the worst-case scenario happened, how could you repair the damage, or to whom might you go for help? To resolve vacation depression, you could fly to a sunnier location. In the case of legal/IRS problems, you could call a lawyer friend for advice about how other people have handled this issue. Ask yourself, "Has anyone less intelligent or less driven than I am faced this same circumstance?" Chances are, the answer is yes.

On a second piece paper, write down this question: "What would be the benefits of an attempt or a partial success?"

List everything that comes to your mind, even if it seems crazy at the time.

On the third paper, write the cost of inaction. What would be the cost of your inaction in all areas of your life—emotionally, physically, financially? Not only right now, but also six months, one year, and three years from now.

When Tim Ferris did this, he realized the atrocious cost of staying at the status quo. When he wrote down in detail what his life would look like, he realized it was a terrifying picture. On a scale of 1 to 10, if he took the trip he was facing a 1 to 3 reversible pain, but an 8 to 10 life-changing impact. So, he took the trip. Nothing bad happened. There were some hiccups, but he even extended his trip. It was the basis of one of his books. He noticed that all the biggest risks averted came from this fear-setting exercise. You can see the Appendix for a worksheet on fear-setting.

THE CHALLENGE

What are the fears that are holding you back from fully living the life God has for you?

CHAPTER 4

SECRET #1

CONTENTMENT

ESAU'S EXAMPLE

Jacob was afraid of the repercussions of his actions so many years ago. God promised Jacob that he would receive the inheritance. But bad things happen when you try to rush ahead of God. Jacob tried to get his birthright through dishonest means.

This lesson appears repeatedly in the Bible. Abraham warned his wife not to tell anyone that she was his wife. He said instead, "Say that you are my sister." Abraham gets himself in trouble, not once but at least twice. Then his son Isaac plays the same thing.

> **If God has called you to do something, He will provide for what he has called you to do.**

Hudson Taylor, the great missionary to China, once said: "God's work, done in God's way will never lack God's supply."[23] Are you content with relying on God? Or do you

---

[23] http://www.leadershipresources.org/the-15-best-james-hudson-taylor-quotes/ Retrieved October 22, 2017

push your own agenda to try to accomplish God's will in your own way and on your timetable?

Jacob was getting ready to meet up with his brother. In fear, he split up his camp, then approached Esau with many gifts. However, God had gone before him and, in a dream, told Esau not to hurt Jacob. When they met, Jacob tried to smooth things over. How did Esau reply? "No, I don't need these gifts. I have enough." Esau did not covet Jacob's possessions. Esau did not need Jacob to supply him with riches because he was already rich. Esau didn't need Jacob's possessions to pacify him. He was reconciled.

The Bible doesn't say many good things about Esau. It talks about his lack of self-control in selling his birthright and going against his parents' advice in the choice of a wife. His family became the Edomites, and for generations, they fought with the Israelites.

Esau did have his flaws, but we see in this instance the power of saying, "I have enough."

THE COMPARING GAME

How much is enough?

How much money is enough?

How many friends do you need before you can say that you have enough?

George Bernard Shaw said, "Money is worth nothing to the man who has more than enough."

Psalm 112:3 says, "Wealth and riches will be in his house, and his righteousness endures forever." The Strong's Concordance comments on this passage tell us that wealth is also translated as "enough".

When God gives us wealth, he gives us enough, sufficient for our needs.

Wealth is viewed from a holistic perspective in the Hebrew mind; it not only includes money but includes physical strength.

Rachel Cruze, the daughter of Dave Ramsey, wrote a book titled "Love Your Life, Not Theirs". In it, she warns about the dangers of comparing your life to that of other people. We look at social media. On Instagram, people post awesome pictures from their dream vacation. But too often, behind the pictures are the fights when they realize they can't afford the credit card bills associated with it.

A friend just posted a picture of his new truck on Facebook, and you think, "Oh, if only I could be that successful!" But you don't see the truth. You don't see his stress and fatigue that came as a result of spending money—that was not his to spend—to impress people who aren't even real friends. We only see a small slice of someone's life. Things are not always as they appear.

Rachel Cruze says, "We need to quit the comparisons, reframing the way you think about money, and developing new habits like avoiding debt, living on a plan, watching your spending, saving for the future, having healthy conversations about money, and giving."[24]

Purchases are often made not because of need, but because of want.

---

[24] Cruz, Rachel. "Love Your Life, Not Theirs". Ramsey Press. 2016.

How much is enough?

Ask a person who is working three jobs to support a family.

Ask a person who is living on the street. They have two different perspectives on the difference between needs and wants.

How much is enough?

Esau was able to say, "I have enough."

Can you say the same thing?

But if only I had a new truck! If only I had a new guitar!

Awww . . . call the "Waaaaaaambulance".

I worked as an Emergency Medical Technician on an ambulance, and we had code words for people like that. We called them "Code Lavenders". They were not really ill, they just wanted attention.

"I want that."

The three most powerful words in the English language.

The three most destructive words in the English language. But "I want that."

How much is enough? When will you believe that you have enough?

THE "THNEED"

Dr. Seuss, in the Lorax, reminds us of the Thneed, which is something that we think that we need. Philippians 4:11 says, "Not that I speak in regard to need, for I have learned in whatever state I am, to be content." Have you learned to be content with your life?

In high school, my friend Matt played the drums and I played guitar. Oh, if only I had something that could amplify the sound of my acoustic guitar! If only I had something like that, so I could hear myself playing. What young guitar player doesn't dream of making it big with music, going on tours with his band, and writing music!

Matt only had one volume when playing the drums, and that was LOUD. So, I thought about it, saved my money, and was able to justify in my mind that if only I had an electric guitar, I could play music with my friend more often. So, I bought it.

Do you know what? I never played my electric guitar with Matt while he played the drums again. We were still friends, but we just never found the time. I spent hundreds of dollars because I thought that what I had wasn't enough. But when I got that electric guitar, I learned that it really wasn't at all necessary.

A few years later, I got interested in amateur radio, where you can talk to people around the world or in your own neighbourhood. I used it to help with emergency communication drills and to connect with my community. Now, if only I had a better amateur radio—not just a new radio, but the best radio I could find! It would be more helpful in connecting with people and with my amateur radio club in Georgia. I thought about it until I was able to justify it. So, I bought a new Kenwood tri-band handheld amateur radio. It was a beauty.

Within a couple of months, I moved away, and I never did get to use that radio to connect with the people who I had originally intended to talk with.

If I am buying something to impress someone, it will never work out.

No, it just never works out. I can justify my purchases. I can rationalize them. But at the end of the day, it's because "I want this" that I make these foolish decisions.

ASK YOURSELF, WHY?

If you are debt-free and if you are generous to God and to others, it's OK to have nice things. But first, figure out why you want to get it. And don't ask why just one time. Ask that question at least five to seven times. Why do you want that purchase? Why do you need it? Why is it important? Why would you do that? If you ask multiple times and explore all the layers, eventually you will get to the root reason.

Let me give you an example. I wanted that electric guitar to play with my friend. Why? I wanted to play music and connect with him. Why? I felt that I didn't have a lot of good friends in high school. Why? I was socially awkward. Why? Naturally, I am a shy person.

60

I discovered the real reason why I wanted that guitar by not being content with superficial answers. If I realize the root values behind a purchase, I can make a decision based on my values. Rather than make the toddler's excuse of "I want this now because I want it now."

WHAT BRINGS YOU JOY?

How much is enough? What would "enough" look like? Is it having more stuff? Less stuff?

In her book, "The Life-Changing Magic of Tidying Up," Marie Kondo talks about the blessing of simplifying.

When we simplify what we have—getting rid of clothes, books, papers, and even keepsakes—we place more value on the small number of possessions we have.

We keep only the things that truly bring us happiness and joy.

Simplifying our lives becomes an amazing thing that will transform every area of our lives, from relationships to finances to diet, even our walk with God.

When we declutter our lives, the Holy Spirit has more power to work in our minds.

"Now godliness with contentment is great gain. For we brought nothing into *this* world, *and it is* certain we can carry nothing out. And having food and clothing, with these we shall be content." (1 Timothy 6:6, 7).

"Godliness with great contentment is great gain." Or, some translations use "great profit". Are we content? Do we have enough? I've never seen a hearse towing a U-Haul truck. We brought nothing into the world. And it is certain we can take nothing out of it. What will make the greatest impact on the world? What will have the greatest impact, not only for here and now, but for eternity? Where is your desire? Where is your love?

Paul says, in Matthew 6:25-26, that if we have the basic necessities of food and clothing, we should be content. "Therefore, I say to you, do not worry about your life, what you will eat or what you will drink; nor about your body, what you will put on. Is not life more than food and the body more than clothing? Look at the birds of the air, for they neither sow nor reap nor gather into barns; yet your heavenly Father feeds them. Are you not of more value than they?" The passage goes on to say, "So do not worry, saying, 'What shall we eat?' or 'What shall we drink?' or 'What shall we wear?' For the pagans run after all these things, and your heavenly Father knows that you need them."

God provides for our necessities and sometimes, God will use your employer to provide for those needs.

Remember Ethan and Emma from the introduction to this book? They never were able to make ends meet. In fact, the hemorrhaging in their financial lives was affecting every other area of their lives. The interesting thing was that they had the newest iPhone, the latest iPad Pro, and drove a more expensive car than I did (well, that wouldn't take much!), yet they didn't have enough money to pay for food for their kids. They had money for toys but seemed to run short when it came to providing the necessities of life.

Epicurus said, "Do not spoil what you have by desiring what you have not; but remember that what you now have was once among the things you only hoped for."[25] How quickly we forget how far we have come! We get a pay raise, and now that is our new normal; we wonder how we ever made it before this raise.

SELL ALL THAT HAS YOU

"If riches increase, do not set your heart on them." (Psalm 61:10). Or, as the New Living Translation says,

"If your wealth increases, don't make it the center of your life."

Who controls who? Money makes a good servant, but a poor master. And money can control you, no matter your income level or the number in your bank account.

"He who loves silver will not be satisfied with silver; Nor he who loves abundance, with increase. This also *is* vanity." (Ecclesiastes 5:10).

---

[25] http://www.quotationspage.com/quote/2431.html retrieved October 22, 2017

Those who seek only to acquire money will never be satisfied with money.

> **Money is a necessity in our world today. God expects us to manage it responsibly, rather than to be controlled by it.**

Christ was approached by a rich young man who asked, "What must I do to inherit eternal life." Christ responded by listing the Ten Commandments, but only the commandments that dealt with mankind—don't steal, don't kill, and don't lie, to name a few. Christ failed to mention the ones that related to a relationship with God. The rich man responded, "All this I have done since I was a child."

"Then Jesus, looking at him, loved him, and said to him, "One thing you lack: Go your way, sell whatever you have and give to the poor, and you will have treasure in heaven; and come, take up the cross, and follow Me."

But he was sad at this word, and went away sorrowful, for he had great possessions." (Mark 10:21-22).

Christ knew this young man's heart. And without beating around the bush, He touched the root of the young man's question. This passage has always bothered me. For one, it appears to be irresponsible. To give everything is presumptuous. I know people who are dirt poor and go from church to church asking others to support their lack of self-discipline. This passage also bothered me because it contradicted some of the other wealth-building principles found in the Bible.

Recently, I heard a talk by Julian Archer, who commented that instead of "Sell all that you have", a better translation would be "Sell all that has you". What possession controls you?

In Matthew 19:23-24, "Then Jesus said to His disciples, 'Assuredly, I say to you that it is hard for a rich man to enter the kingdom of heaven. And again, I say to you, it is easier for a camel to go through the eye of a needle than for a rich man to enter the kingdom of God.'"

The eye of the needle is a term for the gate entering the city. A camel would have to kneel to fit through the narrow gate into the city, shedding its saddles and baggage.

What baggage do you need to get rid of before you can enter the kingdom? Relationships that God has asked you to give up? A particular hobby that God has asked you to give up? A financial idol? Anything that we place in front of God is an idol. And God forbids idol worship. What are you worshiping?

BUDGETING

The Space Shuttle Challenger was made from a million pieces, beautifully crafted and fitting together perfectly. All of them worked together for the Challenger to lift off into space. Over a million pieces of finely-tuned machinery worked together. However, a single o-ring was found to be the cause of the demise of the shuttle and its crew. 99.9999% of the Challenger shuttle worked flawlessly, but that one tiny defective part was fatal. It's the little things in life that make all the difference.

Perhaps there are little things in your life that have been causing you to miss out on the wealth that you could be building. Maybe you've identified those things through reading this book so far. If not, keep reading. There are still a few key points we need to cover that will influence your wealth-building.

Ignas Phillip Semmelweiss, a 19th-century surgeon, found many of his obstetrics patients in Vienna were dying and he didn't know why. His observation soon revealed that those women who were coming down with fevers and subsequently dying were patients who had been seen by doctors who had just performed autopsies on deceased people. Semmelweiss theorized that something was being carried from the morgue to the postpartum ward and that was killing his patients. He encouraged the doctors under his command to wash their hands in a chlorinated lime solution after visiting the morgue and before attending to other patients. When they complied, the infection and fevers were eliminated.

However, Semmelweiss was criticized and mocked by his peers. Ultimately, he suffered a breakdown and was taken to a mental hospital where he died. It was years later, through the work of Pasteur and Lister, that Semmelweiss' theories were validated. It is the little things—often things you can't see—that sometimes have the greatest impact on our lives.

An effective budget must consider the little things. Dave Ramsey says, "A budget is telling your money where to go instead of wondering where it went."

> "*There is* desirable treasure,
> And oil in the dwelling of the wise,
> But a foolish man squanders it."
> (Proverbs 21:20).

There is wealth among both the wise and the foolish. Even though this verse doesn't say it, we could speculate that even if the wise and the foolish made the same amount of money every year, this passage would apply.

The wise person invests in things that have lasting value and focuses on more than just a temporal want.

But a foolish man spends what he has, and then wonders where it went.

When we realize how much is enough, budgeting becomes easier. When we realize that it is not about how much we make, but about how much of that we can invest and give, it changes our financial outlook.

> ## "Everyone thinks of changing the world, but no one thinks of changing himself."
> ## – Leo Tolstoy[26]

If we want to change the world, we must change our own habits first. If we don't have control of our money, our money will control us. Having a budget means accounting for the little things, being consistent, and showing self-control.

"Most people overestimate what they can do in a day, and underestimate what they can do in a month. We overestimate what we can do in a year, and underestimate what we can accomplish in a decade." "The Long View" by Matthew Kelly[27]

---

[26] https://www.goodreads.com/quotes/12841-everyone-thinks-of-changing-the-world-but-no-one-thinks accessed on October 25, 2017

[27] https://www.goodreads.com/quotes/7589545-most-people-overestimate-what-they-can-do-in-a-day accessed on October 25, 2017

What would happen if you made a commitment to long-term financial wellness?

"Wellness" is a term that is in vogue today. It talks about a complete picture. Have you ever done a "complete picture" look at your finances? How close are you to financial wellness?

It starts now. Sit down and start writing a plan for your money. Create a budget for next month using the expenses of this past month as a guide. If you are married, sit down with your spouse and write it together. Then, at the end of your month, compare your actual expenses with what you had planned to spend. The first two or three months may be a bumpy ride and you may have differences of opinion, but this is part of the process. It will get easier.

The first thing to put in your budget is what is called the four walls. These are the housing expenses (including utilities), transportation, food, and basic clothing. You will want to evaluate each of these categories by asking: Am I happy with this amount? In some budget items, and in life,

71

you might realize that spending more on this doesn't lead to a happier life, so why are you doing it? Ask, "If this is not bringing me joy, do I need to cut back in this area?"

There are a couple of things I have found that make budgeting easier.

#1: There's an app for that.

From everydollar.com to mint.com, there are a lot of options to choose from. For many years, I would write a budget in an Excel spreadsheet. The nice thing about an app is that once you make your budget, you can add your expenses when you are on the go. Eventually, it will become a habit. You go to the mall, pay for something, and put it in your app on your phone right there. Right away, you can see how much money you have left in your account.

#2: Pay yourself first.

If you are in debt, you need to pay off your debt first. If you are out of debt, you should schedule an automatic deduction from your checking account into your investments and savings. My friend David does this; he has

20 different online accounts where he distributes his money automatically at the first of the month. He has an account for vacation, children's education, food, etc.

#3 Automate your life.

I personally automate my bills, so I never forget to pay them. Also, I recommend that you look at your online statements at least once a month to catch any wrong charges and monitor for identity theft.

#4 Pay for everything with cash.

I know it's a foreign concept—most people enjoy the convenience of swiping their card, and I just wrote about automating your life! When you pay with cash, you will spend less. The old-fashioned way is to use envelopes. The idea is that every month, you put money into your designated envelope for spending in that area. When I was an adolescent, I would get an allowance and I had an envelope for model railroading and one for Legos. Each envelope was for one of my hobbies. I was purposeful about my money. I spent money differently when it was cash vs. credit. Try it for a short period of time and find out for yourself.

FINANCIAL FREEDOM

How do you define Financial Freedom?

Perhaps you are reading this and thinking of the bill collectors calling to repossess your car. You believe that if you could just pay off that debt, you would be exhilarated! Perhaps you realize that you are running out of money before the end of every month. Your financial life is hemorrhaging, and you need to clot this wound before you bleed out. It is an emergency! I am not exaggerating.

Perhaps you have clawed your way past this stage and you are planning for the future. You see financial freedom as showing generosity, going on nice vacations, and sending your kids to college debt-free.

Your picture of financial freedom may vary at different times in your life. But the basic principles of spending less than you make, investing, getting out of debt, and being generous are the same.

About two years ago, my view of financial independence changed. I was already following Dave Ramsey's principles and his Baby Steps that we will talk about soon. But my perspective changed. Let's just say I discovered how to get FIRE'd. FIRE'd stands for Financial Independence Retire Early. It was birthed from the book, "Your Money or Your Life" by Vicki Robin and Joe Dominguez. Their basic principle is a Biblical principle:

> **"Why do you spend money for what is not bread, and your wages for what does not satisfy?" (Isaiah 55:2).**

I first learned about FIRE'd from Mr. Money Mustache. He finished college debt-free and then set the goal of retiring at age 30. He and his wife both had good jobs as computer programmers, and they lived super-frugally and invested the difference. They had a goal, and they focused on it with laser intensity. Just before the age of 30, they discovered that they had enough money coming in from their investments that they no longer needed to work for an income. Does he still work to earn money? Yes, but he is doing passion projects now, projects he enjoys, and these projects are benefiting his community.

Does he live extravagantly? No, he doesn't. For many years, he didn't have a car and preferred to bike everywhere. His residual income was $25,000 a year. But he had a debt-free house. He has Financial Independence. He has Financial Freedom! He has kept his expenses low, but he is extravagant on those things that are satisfying to him, such as good food cooked at home.

Tim, from Saskatchewan, is another person who started following this philosophy and retired at age 39. He realized that he didn't really enjoy the job he was doing, and it was time for a change. With that same laser focus, he started saving and cutting expenses. He figured that if you can live on 50% of your income, you can retire in 15 years. If you can live on 35% of your income and invest the difference, you can retire in 10 years.[28]

Derek Sivers, in his book "Anything You Want", describes his business success with CD Baby. When he decided it was

[28] https://globalnews.ca/news/3774723/retire-at-35/

time to sell his company, he put all the money in a trust that pays him 5% per year until he dies. Then, that amount will go to music education. He doesn't have a car, a house, or a TV. He has learned how much is enough, and he enjoys the simple things in life.

Rich Mullins, the late Christian music artist, had a similar story. He wrote many praise songs that are now considered Christian classics. He was a humble man who put all his income in a trust to teach music education to kids on a Native reserve. He only asked that the trust would pay him the meager amount his local pastor made. Rich Mullins used his money to be a blessing to others and he enjoyed the simple things in life.

The interesting thing about those people who are FIRE'd is that many of them, without having to worry about a paycheck, have now made more money than they did in their working lives. They are working on their passion projects without the stress of thinking about a salary. They are generous with donating their time and money to the community around them.

In his book, "Change Your Habits, Change Your Life", Tom Corley encourages each reader to write a letter to his or her future self. Where do you want to be five or ten years down the road? Write it down in third person. Dream about where you want to be, and write down goals to support those dreams. Then ask yourself, what habits would support those goals? If your dream is to run a marathon, your first goal might be to start running three miles a day for two weeks, then up the mileage. Your new daily habit will become waking up at 6 a.m. to run for 45 minutes to accomplish a goal that is in line with your dream.

DREAM => GOALS => HABITS

THE CHALLENGE

Stop for a moment and dream. What would Financial Independence look like for you?

1. Do you want to travel the world? Live in a debt-free home? Retire early?

2. What would it take for you to get there? What goals can you set right now?

3. What must you change in your life to meet those goals?

4. What daily habits do you need to follow to achieve your dream?

CHAPTER 5

SECRET #2

FREEDOM FROM DEBT

DEBT IS AN EMERGENCY

They were a group of young people who weren't content seeing the idolatry around them, and they flocked to Elijah and the School of the Prophets. So much so that they had to expand their building, and construction began. Their goal was to build an extension onto the school so that they could learn about God. All the students helped by chopping trees and sawing logs.

However, one young man didn't have his own axe, so he borrowed one. What happened? The axe head came off and landed in the river. He started to stress out—"Oh no, it is a borrowed axe!" We are under obligation to those from whom we borrow things. These young men were working on a righteous activity—building a school to learn about the Lord. But there were still spiritual and emotional consequences for borrowing the axe because he lost something that he had promised to take good care of.

Abraham Lincoln, who would become one of America's greatest presidents, grew up in a poor rural area. He didn't have access to much formal education. He was a self-taught learner who loved to read. He often traveled miles to find someone with a book to borrow. One time, he borrowed a book and accidentally damaged it with water. The owner of the book required three days hard labor to pay for those damages. Lincoln thought his punishment was unfair, but he came away with the idea that he never wanted to be in debt to anyone again.

Proverbs 6 advises that if you have gone into debt to anyone, get out of debt fast; humble yourself before your debt collector. Verse 5 says, "Deliver yourself like a gazelle from the hand *of the hunter*, and like a bird from the hand of the fowler."

Escape like your life depended on it! Like a gazelle being chased like a lion. Because your life depends on it!

"The rich rules over the poor, and the borrower is servant to the lender." (Proverbs 22:7).

In the New International Version, it says that the borrower is a slave to the lender.

How much slavery is OK? Is there a good kind of slavery or a bad kind of slavery? Just like there is good debt and bad debt? Debt is everywhere. Often, it is as commonplace as the family dog underfoot. But I am still looking for a place in the Bible that says financial debt and bondage are a good thing.

Would someone stuck in human trafficking today say it was a good thing? Sex slaves, employees forced to work in sweatshops, child labor? We are appalled by human trafficking, but we turn a blind eye to "modern slavery" and excuse it as "everyone else is doing it." The Bible says that debt is slavery.

> # It's time to declare an emancipation proclamation with your personal finances.

A health reformer in the early 20th century advised: "Shun the incurring of debt as you would shun leprosy."[29]

What is leprosy? It is a bacterial infection that can cause permanent damage to skin, nerves, limbs, and eyes. This can lead to fingers and toes becoming shortened and deformed as cartilage is absorbed into the body.[30]

---

[29] White, Ellen. Councils on Stewardship, Pacific Press, 2010 p 272.

[30] https://en.wikipedia.org/wiki/Leprosy retrieved October 5, 2017

Is leprosy really something you want? Shun debt like slavery. Shun debt like leprosy. Both are things that I would rather stay away from.

The Bible does speak about debt being a good thing but in only one area. Romans 13:8 says, "Owe no one anything except to love one another, for he who loves another has fulfilled the law."

Many people find that the best way to get out of debt is through plastic surgery. You need to cut up those credit cards. When you pay cash for something, you will spend less money. Often, a response to that suggestion is, "But I get points." Have you ever heard a wealthy individual say, "I built my wealth with the points system?" A credit card company realizes it will be making money, or else they wouldn't offer you their card.

EMOTIONAL CONSEQUENCES

I could list statistics about the massive number of people who are drowning in credit card and student loan debt, but most people realize there is a problem.

However, many don't realize the effect that debt has on a person.

Kristen Kuchar wrote about the emotional effects of debt.[31] She commented that while we can argue the virtues of good debt and bad debt, the truth is that any debt has serious emotional and psychological consequences. Countless studies have shown that debt can lead to depression, anxiety, resentment, and denial. Regret, shame, embarrassment, fear, anger, and frustration are a few other perks that you receive when you go into debt. Do any of these sound like the fruit of the Spirit? No, they don't.

A study from the University of Nottingham found that those who struggle to pay off their debts are more than

---

[31] https://www.thesimpledollar.com/the-emotional-effects-of-debt/ retrieved October 5, 2017

twice as likely to experience many health problems, including depression and severe anxiety.[32]

It can also lead to increases in smoking and obesity, which lead to a host of other health challenges.

SPIRITUAL CONSEQUENCES

Few people realize that there are spiritual consequences of debt.

> **Debt is saying, "I am going to put my trust in someone other than God. I don't have to pray about this problem anymore because I can put it on my Visa."**

If a friend loans you money, there is a tendency not to be 100% honest with them because you feel an obligation. This will subtly bring you into dishonesty and lies.

---

[32] http://onlinelibrary.wiley.com/doi/10.1111/j.1468-0297.2012.02519.x/abstract retrieved October 5, 2017

Staying out of debt requires self-discipline. Hebrews 11:24 says that Moses forsook pleasures for a time when he was in Egypt because he kept his eyes on a greater reward. Debt encourages us to covet what other people have. And that is something the Ten Commandments strictly address.

Often, we justify our debt, saying, "I deserve this. I've worked hard for this."

Some people justify debt as retail therapy. Getting nice things is not bad. But when you buy stuff on credit when you can't pay, or if you feel that you are entitled to something just because you work hard, you are being deceived by the enemy!

We should work hard because it is the right thing to do, not because we will be able to spoil ourselves at the end. The three most used—and so very abused—words in the human language are not "I love you". They are, "I want that". Though most often, it sounds like "I waaaaaant that!" said in a whiny three-year-old voice.

You can get into debt by accident, but you can't get out of debt by accident.

THE GOOD DEBT MYTH

Debt consolidation programs don't work. Consolidation is when you roll all your debts into one larger debt. Many times, a lower interest rate is promised. You haven't really changed anything, but you feel good about lower payments. Statistics show that 80% of people who use these services will go back into debt.

Frank lived in a small town in California. He took 10 years to get out of debt by using debt consolidation services. Money fights with his wife were constantly painful for those 10 long years. He became debt-free in January. Oh, the freedom he felt after all those years of fighting! The relief he felt after 10 years of hard work! But within six months, he took out a loan for a car because he just had to have a new car. His habits had not changed, and he slid back into debt.

I have a pastor friend, Steve, who bought a house because those are the things that adults do. Then, he moved to another town. He tried to sell the house, but he couldn't, not after one year, two years, and more. During this time, he shared with me his struggles in his spiritual walk with God because of this large debt.

All debt involves risk, and there are spiritual consequences.

Even a home mortgage has spiritual and emotional consequences. The term mortgage literally means "death contract", but please don't wait till you are dead to pay it off. Look at an amortization schedule and you will see the thousands of dollars you can save by paying it off early.

Most people either have bought or plan to buy a house. It is commonly recommended that you should plan to stay in the area for five to seven years to break even on your purchase.

Chris, a pastor friend from Texas, owned a house, but he was called to move to another church. He soon found that he couldn't find a buyer for the house. Two months of not being able to sell it or rent it out turned into two years. Chris shared with me: "This is really affecting my walk with God. I can't afford to pay for two houses." This same story has repeated itself with multiple pastors that I know.

Yes, there are serious spiritual consequences for debt.

Home ownership also has many hidden costs. Taxes, maintenance costs, closing fees, and mortgage insurance are just a few of the expenses that many people don't factor in. The actual cost of owning a home is much more than most people realize. Don't drink the Kool-Aid.[33] If you had to buy a home without a mortgage, could you do it? Yes. You might just have to get creative.

In his book, "The Wealthy Renter", Alex Avery presents the unique idea that you will get ahead financially if you rent instead of buying. It does take self-discipline to invest the money that you normally put toward a house.

Another good debt that people might try to tell you about is education. I believe in getting an education. It's important. A friend of mine, Andrew, went to college to get his degree and racked up a massive amount of student loan debt. After he graduated, he felt God was calling him to be a missionary, and he found a perfect position serving on a Native reserve. However, his prospective employer told him, "I'm sorry, but you can't afford to take this job. You have too much debt, compared with what you will be

---

[33] A reference to Jim Jones and his cult following the suicide.

making." Andrew's debt kept him from serving the Lord completely; instead, he served the master of debt.

In my senior year of high school, I expected to have to take out loans for college. That's what everyone does, right? Kind of like they expect you to get up in the morning and put on a shirt. It's the social norm. Instead, my mom told me, "I went to college debt-free, and you can as well."

"But, Mom, things are different now. You just don't do that now." My mom responded, "I had to work my way through college, and you get to work as well." And Mom was right.

My parents were not making a lot of money, but they believed in me. So, I worked each summer, along with two or three part-time jobs while at college. My parents and grandparents helped, and, by God's grace, we made it—not only once but twice. My sister graduated debt-free from college as well. If my mom hadn't presented the idea of a debt-free education, I would have never considered it.

Many of my college friends also worked several jobs and were able to pay their way through college. Nathan started a lawn mowing business in college and did quite well for himself. Rachelle made handmade Christmas wreaths and baskets.

When I graduated, I was able to take on a missionary position for several years where I gained valuable life and work experiences.

Financial freedom gives you freedom in every area of your life. Financial freedom gives you the ability to make choices. Financial freedom allows you to be generous with your time and money.

Even "safe debt", such as buying a house and going to school, has emotional and spiritual consequences. As we go into "debt slavery", we should count the costs. We need to carefully consider the leprous consequences of accepting a disease into our lives and into our family.

Perhaps people willingly accept the debt bondage without understanding that God really wanted them to trust Him more, ask for His wisdom and guidance, and then become more creative with managing their finances. Perhaps debt is limiting our creativity in finding alternative ways to buy a house or pay for college.

THE CHANGE

Remember the Biblical story of building the School of the Prophets? The young man came to Prophet Elijah and explained the problem—he had borrowed an axe, then he lost the axe head when it flew off into the river.

Let's pick up the story in 2 Kings 6:6-7: "So the man of God said, 'Where did it fall?' And he showed him the place. So, he cut off a stick and threw *it* in there; and he made the iron float. Therefore, he said, 'Pick *it* up for yourself.' So, he reached out his hand and took it."

God wants you to get out of debt. And He will open a way. God may provide a miracle, but most often, getting out of debt requires hard work and determination. "For God has not given us a spirit of fear, but of power and of love and of a sound mind." (2 Timothy 1:7). Another way to translate the words "a sound mind" is to use the word self-discipline.

Self-discipline is a fruit of the Spirit. You can slide into debt without realizing it, but you can't slide out of it. Christ came to set you free—not to put you in bondage. Debt puts us in bondage.

"Therefore, if you have not been faithful in the unrighteous mammon, who will commit to your trust the true *riches?*" (Luke 16:11).

If we can't handle money wisely, the Bible tells us we will not be given deeper and truer riches from heaven.

Dave Ramsey, a Christian financial advisor and a talk show host, has the best methodical plan to get out of debt. Literally millions of people have used this same plan. For a more detailed look at this plan, check out Dave Ramsey's book, "The Total Money Makeover."[34] Here are the Baby Steps that Ramsey recommends:

- Baby Step 1 – $1,000 to start an Emergency Fund.

- Baby Step 2 – Pay off all debt using the Debt Snowball.

- Baby Step 3 – put 3 to 6 months of expenses in savings.

- Baby Step 4 – Invest 15% of household income into pre-tax retirement.

---

[34] Ramsey, Dave. "The Total Money Makeover". Ramsey Press. 2004

- Baby Step 5 – College funding for children.

- Baby Step 6 – Pay off home early.

- Baby Step 7 – Build wealth and give![35]

Imagine if you were completely out of debt.

"What would it feel like if you didn't have a payment in the world?"[35]

You have a debt-free house. You have saved and put your kids through college.

Imagine what you could do for the kingdom of God. Think of Abraham, Isaac, Jacob, Job, David, and Solomon. Think of how Nicodemus helped the early church in its infancy to spread the truth literally unto the ends of the earth. These are Biblical heroes who used their wealth to be a blessing to other people.

---

[35] quote from Financial Peace University

DEBT SNOWBALL

So, you are at a point where you are saying, "Pastor Jonathan, I have a massive amount of debt. I have debt collectors calling me at all hours of the day and night. How do I escape?"

Many people have used the debt snowball as a way to stay motivated throughout the process. Start with the smallest debt first and pay it off. Then, go to your next smallest debt. The logical approach would be to pay off the one with the highest interest rate. You get the most psychological win when you pay off the smallest debt first. You can write it off forever, and not have to go back to it!

For motivation, it's better to pay them off smallest to largest. First, list your debts from smallest to largest. Make minimum payments on the rest of your bills and pay off that smallest bill as fast as possible. Once that debt is gone, take that payment and roll it into your next smallest debt. Repeat, repeat, repeat and watch your snowball gain momentum as it rolls down the hill.

Let's give a quick example.

Credit card 1 – $400 at 11% with a monthly payment of $25.

Credit card 2 – $1,000 at 18% with a monthly payment of $50.

Car loan – $6,000 at 4% over four years with a monthly payment of $135.

Student loan – $15,000 at 5% over 10 years with a monthly payment of $159.

If you pay the minimum payments on everything and add an extra $100 to the smallest credit card payment, you'll pay it off in four months. Next, go after the second credit card with $175 per month. Where did that money come from? Well, $100 plus the newly freed-up $25, plus the $50 payment you're already making. This one will also be gone in five months. Now you have $310 a month ($175 plus $135) to put toward the car! Watch that auto loan go away in 15 months. By the time you get to the student loan, you'll be paying $469 on it each month! With focused intensity, you can be completely debt-free in a couple of years.[36]

Christ came to set you free. "He came to give you life, and life more abundantly."[37]

> **God cares not only about your spiritual freedom, but about your physical health, your financial health, and the health of your relationships.**

He doesn't want us to serve any other gods.

But when we are in debt, someone else gets to call the shots.

---

[36] http://startuup.co/pay-off-debt-debt-snowball-plan/ retrieved October 5, 2017

[37] John 10:10

THE CHALLENGE

Is it your desire today to only serve God, and have no other gods before you? Do you want the freedom that Christ offers in the form of financial freedom?

CHAPTER 6

SECRET #3

FAITHFULNESS

WINTER IS COMING

My phone rang and when I answered, an elderly lady asked, "Can you help me with rent? I am a retired lawyer. I helped a lot of people and volunteered my services to the less fortunate. Now I can't pay my rent."

As I chatted with her, she shared that she had made more than $100,000 a year in her professional career, but she hadn't planned for retirement. "I just didn't think I was going to get old," she commented.

She had called the church, hoping to find money for rent. She was going to be evicted from her home at the end of the month. Her retirement income from the government wasn't enough to support her. She was a faithful Christian woman who had failed to faithfully plan for the future.

Proverbs 6:6 reminds us to learn from the ant. The ant collects food in the summer to prepare for winter.

My friends, winter is coming. Winter comes when your car breaks down. Winter comes when you learn that you have lost your job and you don't have an emergency fund to tap during the transition. Winter comes when your kids reach college age—wow, how did they grow up so soon?

Jerry, one of my pastor friends, is extremely generous with his giving to overseas missions. He is generous when it comes to his toy fund. I mean, tools for ministry. You know the old saying, "The difference between men and boys is the price of their toys." But he hasn't yet prepared for retirement. He tells me, "The Lord is coming soon."

I truly believe that, but I also expect that the Lord calls us to be faithful with what He has given us, and "to occupy till He comes".

DILIGENCE

Proverbs 14:24 says, "The crown of the wise is their riches, But the foolishness of fools is folly." The principles for building wealth are in the Bible. But perhaps we run past those 2,400 verses that talk about wealth in our quest to find the 500 verses that talk about love. There are 215 verses related to faith and 218 verses relating to salvation. God has given us wealth and money to test what is in our hearts, and how we can use our wealth and riches to show our love to other people.

> **"The plans of the diligent lead surely to plenty, but those of everyone who is hasty, surely to poverty."**
> **(Proverbs 21:5)**

Slow and steady wins the race. If you are looking for a get-rich-quick scheme, that will lead to you becoming broke. We all have friends who are looking for the next "big deal" that will make them rich. God calls us to be diligent. God calls us to be faithful with the financial resources He has given us. If you are diligent in your saving and investing, you will gain wealth.

If you are diligent in your exercise program you will gain strength and health. Most people don't go from couch potato status to running a marathon in a week or two. You must train for it. You must be diligent—start small and build up from there. If you are diligently caring for your spouse, you will have years of a happy marriage. Faithfulness is a gift of the fruit of the Spirit. When we ask God to send the Holy Spirit into our lives, He will help us with our wealth-building habits.

"The soul of a lazy man desires, and has nothing; but the soul of the diligent shall be made rich." (Proverbs 13:4).

The Bible says we will build wealth when we are diligent with our finances. There is a modern financial term that supports this 2,000-year-old proverb. Dollar-cost averaging is when I diligently put money into my investment account, consistently, every single month. I don't care whether the market goes up or if it goes down. I am diligent, and I will come out ahead financially if I am faithful.

My family personally practices this financial principle. We have a set amount automatically withdrawn from our checking account on the first of each month.

God is calling us to be faithful in our savings, our work ethic, and in our investing.

WORK ETHIC

Remember Jacob from the chapter about having enough? He was in a bind. Something had to change. He felt like he was getting nowhere. In Genesis 30, he asked Laban, his father-in-law, for permission to leave. Laban replied, "Name your wages. I want you to stay because I have learned from experience that God blesses you." When you are working for the Lord and following His plan, He will bless you and bless those around you through your influence.

Jacob then responded to Laban, "Let me take the speckled sheep as my wages." Jacob worked hard, and the Lord blessed him. His flocks increased, and the Bible described him as exceedingly prosperous.

What happens when you work hard? You start seeing success. And others will become jealous. Jacob overheard Laban's sons gossiping: "The only reason that Jacob has become wealthy is because he has taken it from our father." Laban's sons were playing the victim card.

The book "Manufacturing Victims", by Dr. Tana Dineen, talks about the dangers and the self-defeating prophecy if you claim to be a victim vs. claiming to be a victor. Even those who survive dramatic experiences such as the Nazi concentration camps will recover more quickly if they do not view themselves as victims.

Dave Ramsey, in his book "More than Enough", says, "Whining is a sign of a lack of character on your part."[38]

Jacob's brothers-in-law never mentioned anything about God blessing Jacob. They never mentioned anything about the cold nights Jacob spent protecting Laban's sheep. Nary a mention of Jacob's work ethic, or that he was skilled in what he did. Their only comment was, "He stole what he has."

Jealousy and covetousness are often seen today as well. A person will work for 20 years to become the top of his field of study, then a news report will label him as an "overnight success".

---

[38] See page 18 of "More Than Enough"

BUILDING THE SCHOOL OF THE PROPHETS

The children of Israel were at a low point spiritually, and the idolatry of surrounding nations had crept in around them. But there was one bright point. 2 Kings 6 states that the School of the Prophets led by Elijah was bulging at the seams. Elijah had no particular gift for leadership. His strength was in submitting to the Holy Spirit, who is given to everyone who exercises faith.

What did the students do? Those young people saw the need. They also saw the solution, and they weren't afraid of hard work. So, they went out and chopped down trees to build a larger school. Throughout scripture, hard work and manual labor are lifted up and praised.

Christ was a carpenter, Paul a tentmaker, Dorcas was a seamstress. Proverbs 31 describes a woman who "seeketh wool and flax, and worketh willingly with her hands," who "giveth meat to her household, and their task to her maidens," who "looketh well to the ways of her household, and eateth not the bread of idleness."

In fact, Paul says, in 2 Thessalonians 3:10, that if you don't work you shouldn't eat, and you are worse than an unbeliever if you don't provide for your household. The Bible brings out the importance of work. In 2 Kings, we see the benefits of young people working toward a goal.

"Genius is one percent inspiration and ninety-nine percent perspiration. Accordingly, a 'genius' is often merely a talented person who has done all of his or her homework." – Thomas Edison[39]

"Showing up is 80% of life." – Woody Allen[40]

A good, solid work ethic is showing up and giving it your best. Ecclesiastes 9:10 says, "Whatever your hand finds to do, do it with your might." If you are going in, be all in. Get after it as if you were working for God and not for man. Proverbs 22:29 says, "Do you see a man that excels in his work? He will stand before kings; he will not stand before

[39] http://www.thomasedison.com/quotes.html retrieved October 15, 2017

[40] As Woody says, "Showing up is 80 percent of life." https://en.wikiquote.org/wiki/Woody_Allen retrieved October 15, 2017

unknown men." When we have a work ethic and work hard, people will notice. We honour God and can be a witness by our excellent work.

In the book "Disrupt You!", Jay Samit says, "Live a few years of your life in a way most people won't so that you can spend the rest of your life living at a level most probably can't."[41]

Dave Ramsey has a similar quote, "If you will live like no one else, later you can live and give like no one else."[42] This is not just about sacrificing like no one else now to get out of debt. It can be applied also starting a side business.

More than 2,000 years before Dave Ramsey or Jay Samit, the Bible's faith chapter, Hebrews 11, said that Moses forsook pleasures for a time because he saw a greater reward. When applied to your financial life, this principle of self-sacrifice means that you are consistently saving toward that emergency fund or maybe that early retirement dream.

---

[41] http://startupsinnovation.com/jayquotes/ retrieved October 15, 2017

[42] https://twitter.com/DaveRamsey?lang=en retrieved October 15, 2017

You are putting off what feels good now so that you can enjoy your long-term goals. Other people would say you are "adulting it" and not acting like a child.

FAITHFULNESS IN SAVINGS

There is a well-known children's story, that is recommended by multimillionaires, on the secret of building wealth. The story begins with a race between two unlikely and different creatures—a tortoise and a hare. The tortoise slowly plodded over the starting line, one foot in front of the other, faithfully going down the raceway. He was consistent. In contrast, the hare was impatient. He had lots of energy and bounded through the course until he was distracted at a beautiful spot and decided to take a nap. "I am ahead in the race, I can slow down and enjoy myself a little bit," the hare said. So, he slept in the warm sun.

The tortoise didn't stop.

He put one foot in front of the other. He was faithful. He was diligent. He worked on, while the hare slept. The hare finally woke up to the screams and celebrations of one of God's slowest creatures winning the race.

Slow and steady wins the race. Live on less than you make, and you will be amazed at the results of your diligence.

A 2011 study found that a person's savings rate is more important for wealth building than what that person invests in.[43]

What? You mean I don't have to invest in risky investments or look for that hot stock pick? No, it's your savings rate. If you invest 10%, you will be able to retire in 51.4 years. If you can invest 25% of your income, you can retire in 31 years. If you invest 66% of your income, you can retire in 10 years.[44] What is the key? Living on less than you make. Realizing how much is enough.

[43] *David M. Blanchett, QPA, QKA, and Jason E. Grantz, QPA, ASSP Journal, Summer 2011*

[44] https://www.youtube.com/watch?v=7X7wBEezr3g retrieved October 24, 2017

I taught a financial success class at a small Christian high school in Edmonton, Alberta, and the students were amazed when I showed them how compound interest works. They asked multiple times to explain how money can build on itself without a person really doing anything.

Interest is bad when it is on a credit card bill, but it is awesome when you are building wealth.

There are many compound interest calculators online and in apps. Experiment with it and learn the financial benefit of being faithful long-term. In the interest field, money does build upon money.

If you invest $650 a month for 10 years at a 7% interest rate, you will have $114,000. You only put in $78,000 but your money earned $35,000 on your investment. You will find more growth the longer you leave your money in that account and faithfully add to it. In 20 years you will have $341,000; in 30 years, $796,000. Over 30 years' time you have only put in $234,000 of your own money, but you have earned $561,000 in interest! All because of your faithfulness and patience.

Dave Ramsey recommends investing 15% of your income in retirement accounts.

The principle here is to start early and invest often.

Set it up on autopilot so you don't even think about it.

But in a deeper sense, what about your spiritual life? If you faithfully spend time in the Word of God every morning, do you realize the compound interest you could have in 5 years? 10 years? 30 years? It will be amazing!

In many places, the Bible says that the diligent shall be made rich. Does research back this up? In "Change Your Habits, Change Your Life", it says that 80% of self-made millionaires became wealthy after the age of 50. In "The Millionaire Next Door", it says most millionaires take 18 years to reach their first million. Are you willing to be patient? Are you willing to wait for the good stuff? Delayed gratification is good for my two-year-old. It is also good for us adults when it comes to our investing strategy.

FOUR STRATEGIES FOR INVESTING

We have learned that it's not where you put the investments but your savings rate that is the most important thing for building wealth. Here are some simple rules for investing.

#1 Know your risk tolerance.

The basic advice is, don't invest it if you can't lose it. If you are single without kids, you have a different risk threshold than a married couple with a couple of kids. Your current circumstances could affect your comfort level for the risk you are willing to take. If you are married, talk it over with your spouse. You may be on different pages about how risky of an investment you make.

#2 Know what you are investing in.

You are responsible for your money. God has given you the responsibility of being a good steward, and that is why you are investing. Do your research on the company you are thinking about partnering with. How long has it been in business? What has been its 10-year, 15-year, 20-year track record?

Talk to a financial advisor or a fiduciary to help you in the process. A fiduciary is a neutral third party who offers financial advice for a fee; he or she is required to be neutral, but many fiduciaries sell investments as well. A financial advisor makes money by the investments they sell, which isn't a bad thing if you trust your advisor.

At the end of the day, you are still responsible. I talked to Gary, who sells private equities, a kind of investment. He recommended several options. Looking through the fine print with an accountant, I realized that I couldn't even consider at least two of the four recommendations because I was a U.S. citizen living in Canada. You are responsible for your investments, and no one else.

#3 Diversify.

Don't put all your eggs in one basket.

"But divide your investments among many places, for you do not know what risks might lie ahead." (Ecclesiastes 11:2 from the New Living Translation).

If your foreign investments aren't doing well, you need to diversify with other investments that will boost them up.

Mutual funds are automatically diversified, but if you have riskier investments you need to think, about how you can mitigate that risk.

One way to diversify is to have multiple streams of income. You need to develop a side hustle. Not everyone is cut out to be an entrepreneur, but it's always good to have a plan B if your current employer decides there are cutbacks for unknown reasons.

> # There is no one who will have a commitment to take care of you, like you.

The book "Who moved my cheese", by Spencer Johnson, tells a parable about two mice and two little people. It shows the importance of anticipating change, and being able to change. Check out Chris Guillebeau's books, "The $100 Start Up" or "Side Hustle", to start your creative juices going on what you could do for your side business.

#4 Set up your investing to be automatic.

The more you automate your life, the more likely it will happen. I really like the "set it and forget it" model, which means you need to be thinking about buying and holding for the long term. Charles Munger, the silent partner to Warren Buffet, says, "If you only could make 20 investment moves in your entire life, what would they be?" Some people move in and out of investments like they are changing their socks.

Remember Ric Edel's example in "The Truth About Money"? The stock market is like a boy with a yo-yo. If you watch the yo-yo of the stock market too much, you will become fearful and bail out completely. But if you step back, you will notice that while the yo-yo is going up and down, the boy is walking up the hill. We can see the stock market going up and, while there are major corrections in the market (usually every 10 years), the overall trend is upward.

Now, let's get into specific investment vehicles. There are only a few. An index fund is a type of mutual fund with a portfolio that follows the S&P 500 Index. It provides you with diversity in many different sectors of the market while not moving stocks around a lot, and keeps operating expenses low. You will be charged a fee to buy and to sell. Most investment books would recommend this. Check out the books "The Little Book of Common Sense Investing" by John C. Bogle; "A Random Walk Down Wall Street" by Burton G. Malkiel; and "The Little Book That Still Beats the Market" by Joel Greenblatt and Andrew Tobias

One of my friends, John from Arizona, started investing 30 years ago. He and his family were living on a small salary, but he started researching investments that paid dividends on a regular basis, whether the market was up or down.[45] Today, John has a net worth of more than a million dollars. He uses his wealth to be a blessing to his family, church, and the community. One of the best books I have read about this is "The Lazy Investor" by Derek Foster.

Mutual funds are an investment program where people join together to invest in the stock market. The advantage of a mutual fund is that it is a collection of funds, sometimes over 100, with a natural diversification that provides a safety

---

[45] See dripinvesting.org for more information

net. If oil is down one year, you still have investments in utilities.

Many financial books speak negatively about mutual funds because of the fees that are involved. Here are a few things to consider: Studies show that people who use mutual funds and have financial advisors are more confident about their investments and about their retirement. When you are afraid and want to sell everything because of what China (or another country) is doing in the markets, a financial advisor can calm you down and make sure you don't jump off the proverbial cliff and sell everything.

If you want to master any skill—whether running, exercise, or cooking—one of the fastest ways to reach your goal is to pay for a coach, according to Robert Greene's book, "Mastery". Even in writing this book, I have used a coach so that I can do my best in this project. If I would get a coach to achieve my exercise goals, why wouldn't I pay money to get financial advice as well? I believe it is money well spent.

There are many other options for investing. I have included here the most popular and the easiest ones to start.

I encourage you to spend some time going over the four rules of investing, do your research, and then go for it. The ancient proverb is true. The best time to plant a tree is 25 years ago, the next best time to plant a tree is today. I want you to commit today to planting that tree—the money tree that will produce money even when you stop working.

A money tree is not a fictional wish, it is something that takes diligence and long-term planning.

BETTY'S STORY

James loved his Aunt Betty. Aunt Betty was his favourite aunt. She was always generous, and her kindness affected everyone she met. One day, Betty was out-of-town, and James decided to go over and mow her lawn. When he finished mowing, he realized he had forgotten his lunch.

"Not a problem," he thought to himself. "I'll just go in and help myself to the fridge."

James walked into his aunt's house and looked in the fridge. Nothing was there except a few condiments, so he checked

SECRET #3 - FAITHFULNESS

the cupboards. They were bare of everything except one thing. Five cans of dog food. He stopped as the realization sunk in—his aunt didn't have a dog.

It was then that James realized he needed to get his financial house in order. He needed to plan for retirement. He went home and finally got serious about planning for the future.[46]

What about you? Are you ready to get serious about your financial life? Are you ready to apply the fruits of the Spirit, not only in your spiritual life but in your relationships, your health, and your finances? It won't happen by accident. It's not easy, but with determination and the blessing of God, it will happen. The fruit of the Spirit should affect every area of your life. Now get after it.

---

[46] Story used from Chris Hogan's book, "Retire Inspired"

CHAPTER 7

SECRET #4

GENEROSITY

GIVE AWAY THE BEST

Once, there was a farmer who was new to farming. He bought seed and planted and planted. When the harvest finally came, he decided to celebrate, and he enjoyed the largest vegetables at his own table. He knew he had to save for next year, but decided to save the seed from the smallest ones. Next year, he planted those seeds but was disappointed. What grew up was a sorry excuse for a vegetable.

> ## When you plant the smallest, you will reap the smallest.

If you plant seeds from the vegetables and fruit that were the largest, you pass that genetic material on to the next generation. When you take the best for yourself, you are missing out on an abundant harvest for the future.

GAINING WEALTH BY GIVING

As many people will attest, the easiest way to make money is to give it away. Chris Anderson's book, "Free", suggests you look at some of today's largest companies that are successful because they give stuff away. Facebook and Google have given their main platform away for free, and yet they have reaped huge rewards. Free Wi-Fi at coffee shops? Yes, the easiest way to make money is to give it away.

Gary Vaynerchuk's book, "The Thank You Economy", says that people are willing to pay more for something if they get great customer service. A company's generosity may not be monetary. The best thing that they can offer is time and attention to you, the valued customer.

DO NOT TRUST IN RICHES

"Command those who are rich in this present age not to be haughty, nor to trust in uncertain riches but in the living God, who gives us richly all things to enjoy. *Let them* do good, that they be rich in good works, ready to give, willing to share." (1 Timothy 6:17, 18).

God has not called us to trust in our riches but to trust Him, the God in heaven. When we realize that we are merely a steward of God, it changes our attitude and gives us a spirit of gratitude. Why has God given us money? To bless other people. To bring them to the kingdom.

Matthew 5:16 says: "Let your light so shine before men, that they may see your good works and glorify your Father in heaven." God has given us money so that we may do His good works, that we may glorify our Father in heaven.

Matthew 24 talks about the signs of the last days—diseases, wars, famines. We can make a checklist and see this happening. That chapter is followed by Matthew 25, which has parables related to the preceding chapter—the story of the foolish virgins who didn't have extra oil, the parable of the talents, which relates to us using the gifts and money He has given us and multiplying them.

Starting in Matthew 25:31, Christ talks about the judgment, separating the sheep and the goats. His guidelines for His judgment is "For I was hungry, and you gave Me food; I was thirsty, and you gave Me drink; I was a stranger, and you took Me in; I was naked, and you clothed Me; I was sick, and you visited Me; I was in prison, and you came to Me. Then the righteous will answer Him, saying, 'Lord, when did we see You hungry and feed You, or thirsty and give You drink?

When did we see You a stranger and take You in, or naked and clothe You? Assuredly, I say to you, inasmuch as you did it to one of the least of these my brother, you did it to Me."

When you show compassion to those around you, you are doing it to God and not to man. When we spend time on the activities that Christ spent time doing, Matthew 6:20 tells us we are building up treasure in heaven where moth and rust do not destroy.

How we spend our money and our time will affect whether we are considered a sheep or a goat.

THE WORLD GIVES TO GIVERS

"There is a severe evil *which* I have seen under the sun: Riches kept for their owner to his hurt." (Ecclesiastes 5:13).

"The world gives to givers, and takes from takers." We see this in the story of the parable of the talents. The one servant who hid his talent instead of investing it? His talent was taken away from him.

As a pastor, I felt a conviction to start thanking people more from the front of the church and to give them a little thank you from our family in the form of a gift card and a handwritten note. I was amazed when, around that same time, my wife needed a new sewing machine, went into Walmart, and found that the sewing machine was steeply discounted. Do you know what? It was discounted by the same amount that I had just given away. The more we are generous with other people, the more God can be generous with us.

> ## John Wesley once commented, "Make all you can, save all you can, give all you can."

It seems like an oxymoron, but it is also a statement about balance. It's a statement that our priorities should be thinking not only of ourselves and the present but long-term thinking about what will be a blessing to other people. There will be times in your financial journey when you need to clean up your own mess and get out of debt before you are able to help someone else. Every time I fly, I am reminded of that same message: "In the event of cabin pressure loss, please put your oxygen mask on first, and then help those around you with their masks."

We become financially independent, we can be a blessing to other people. Imagine having the finances to support missionaries overseas or at home. Not just a little bit here or there, but giving large amounts. Of seeing a need in your church and community and being able to help. Because God has blessed you, you can be a blessing to other people.

Sarah was in school in Nevada and was struggling financially. I was impressed by God to give her a large amount of money. Truth be told, it was the largest gift I had ever given, but I talked with my wife and she was on the same page. We sent a check and didn't hear anything for several days. Then, Sarah called. She was in tears. She'd had pennies in her account, and this check meant a lot to her family.

Omer Redden's book, "Give and Grow Rich," says, "Every rich man I know is generous. Generous with his money, generous with his time, or generous with the wages he gives.

Rich men know that the key to getting rich is giving. Look at what God has done for you and for me, sending His Son to die on the cross. Look at the countless times we have seen in Scripture and in our own personal lives how He pursues and loves and forgives. That sets the precedent for how we should give. God is an extravagant giver. Are you?"

ALL THAT IS NOT GIVEN AWAY IS LOST

It was the last day of my mission trip to Tanzania. We had just finished presenting Bible and health meetings for several communities. I was one of the sponsors of the trip. Some of the students on the trip gave away all their possessions just before leaving. "I can get more in the states when I return," they reasoned. "Why not be generous with what I have?"

I had a different attitude. "I don't want to give away dirty socks." I wanted to give them something that they would value, so I justified my decision. I knew that the local missionaries really valued "Back to Eden", a book about natural remedies. I decided that I would give them this book.

We flew back to the U.S. As we waited for our luggage, the carousel came around once, came around twice. Everyone collected their luggage, and I was the only one without my bag. It started to sink in. I had traveled many times internationally, but this was the first time the airline had lost my bag. I went to file my claim with the airline.

Over the next few days, God spoke to me.

I had only lost the things that I had not given away.

The book that I was generous with was something I had not lost. "He is no fool who gives what he cannot keep to gain that which he cannot lose."[47] All that is not given away is lost.

---

[47] Jim Elliot, missionary to Ecuador,

https://www.goodreads.com/author/quotes/2125255.Jim_Elliot

CHAPTER 8

THE LAUNCHING PAD

This is not the conclusion, as you may find in some books. This is merely the beginning.

The beginning of you handling God's money differently.

The beginning of realizing what is enough.

The beginning of getting out of debt.

The beginning of being diligent and making long-term plans with your money.

The beginning of being generous.

This is the beginning of discovering Biblical wealth.

Each of these money habits is interconnected.

If you give without planning for retirement, you will get into trouble.

If you realize what is enough, and yet are not generous, you will not have a satisfying life.

Congratulations. You have made it where some people never go. Many people never get to the end of the book they start, but you have.

"But Jesus said to him, 'No one, having put his hand to the plow, and looking back, is fit for the kingdom of God.'" (Luke 9:62).

And now, here you are. You have determined that you will think and act differently when it comes to money.

These are Biblical principles. These are universal principles that God has put in His Word. They are principles that, if applied to your finances, will help you build wealth.

What is wealth? It is realizing what is enough. It is getting out of debt, and then investing for the future. It is practicing generosity because you have a vision of a larger goal. You will spend the future being a blessing to those around you. This is what Biblical wealth is.

Where do you go from here? The average millionaire reads one nonfiction book a month. I want to encourage you to read as well. Most of this book is the result of my reading other financial books, taking notes, and compiling those notes. Here are a few book recommendations that will expand your view of personal finance.

"The Richest Man in Babylon" by George Clausen. This book presents the basic concepts of personal finance using fun, adventurous stories. Outside of the Bible, this is probably the oldest personal finance book, but it is still relevant today.

"The Total Money Makeover" by Dave Ramsey. If you are struggling with debt, Ramsey is your man. He has created an international brand based on getting people out of debt and giving hope to people about dealing with their money. His Baby Steps are the most logical approach to personal finance. Check out his podcast as well. You will be blessed.

In, **"Change Your Habits, Change Your Life"**, Tom Corley interviewed 177 millionaires and found some interesting habits that they had in common. I don't care if I ever become a millionaire, but if I follow the habits of successful people, I will also become successful.

"Retired Inspired" by Chris Hogan. A powerful book about planning for retirement. Hogan is a Dave Ramsey speaker and does a good job of starting off with the driving motivation for you to plan for retirement.

"The Compound Effect" by Darren Hardy. This book shows the value of developing habits that, if continued over the long term, will lead to incredible results. It takes faithfulness and persistence, but if you continue at them you will receive amazing results. If your "reason why" is big enough, you can accomplish anything.

There are many more excellent books on finances, but there are other books that will distract you from your goals. Choose wisely.

I want you and your family to be intentional about using God's money. Start making a financial plan. Make a budget. Plan for your future. Commit to following a Biblical pathway.

I would be remiss if I only expressed concern for your personal financial life. There is something else that I want you to consider.

There is something more important than your planning for retirement.

There is something even more important than being able to meet your expenses month-to-month.

There is something more important than being intentional about your money.

What's more important?

Your Eternal Salvation

What good would it be to gain the whole world, to make all sorts of money, then lose your relationship with Jesus?[48]

Spending time with Jesus every morning will have a more valuable compound effect than the hottest investment. Daily personal devotions will set your course for eternity.

If you ever need help in the process of developing a deeper walk with God or finances, feel free to email me.

I pray that you will live a life of outrageous generosity through self-discipline.

Blessings,

Pastor Jonathan Geraci
info@wealthbuildingsecrets.net

---

[48] Mark 8:36 paraphrase

APPENDIX

ABOUT THE AUTHOR

Jonathan Geraci resides in Yellowknife, Northwest Territories, Canada. He is the pastor of a church located 400 kilometers (250 miles) south of the Arctic Circle. He is married with two small children and enjoys being active outdoors, getting involved in the community, and teaching about Biblical financial principles.

Contact Pastor Jonathan to book a weekend Wealth Building Secrets Seminar in your local church or community.

ACKNOWLEDGMENTS

There are many people who made this book possible. First, my wife and kids. Thank you for being supportive of Daddy's crazy ideas. Thank you.

From the Self-Publishing School training and community: my writing coach, Scott Allen; my accountability partner, Susan McLaughlin; Samantha Adrianne Photography, who did an awesome last-minute photo shoot; and my editors, Twyla Geraci and Wendy Smith. Thank you all for the part you played in making this book a success.

To my incredible launch team. You helped make this book possible. Thank you!

For our creator, God, who loves us and cares for us in ways we can hardly imagine.

Thank you.

FEAR-SETTING WORKSHEET

"We suffer more often in imagination than in reality."
—*Seneca*

1. Define what you fear. What is the worst-case scenario?

2. How could you prevent, or at least minimize, the risk of these things happening?

3. If the worst-case scenario did happen, how could you repair the damage? To whom could you go for help?

4. What might be the benefits of an attempt or a partial success?

5. What would the cost of inaction be—emotionally, physically, financially, family, etc.—in six months, one year, and three years from now?

6. On a scale of 1-10, rank the pain scale for each of these. (10 being the worst pain)

7. On a scale of 1-10, rank the life-changing impact.

THE SEVEN TIPS TO ATTEND COLLEGE DEBT-FREE

1. Choose a degree where you know you can get a job ahead of time; don't get a degree without a solid career outlook. We all know people who have gotten degrees such as the proverbial underwater basket weaving. When they graduate, they wonder why they can't find a job. Remember the carpenter's mantra, "Measure twice, cut once."

2. Career-shadow a place you might want to work in the future. While you are there, ask yourself if you are excited about this career field and could commit to doing this for the foreseeable future. It's better to find out now, rather than in four years when you graduate.

3. Score well on your SATs and ACTs. Spend time taking classes and reading well to take these tests. The better you

do on these tests, the more college scholarships you will receive.

4. Make it your full-time job to apply for grants and scholarships. The Free Application for Federal Student Aid, or FASFA, grants are based on financial need. Some are also based on your career path. Just read the fine print, sometimes they will offer loans as well.

Many companies are offering free money if you just ask. Go to your future employer and see if they will sponsor you to go to school in agreement that you will work for them afterward.

5. Start a side hustle business while in high school and college. Check out Chris Guillebeau's books, "The $100 Start Up" or "Side Hustle", to start your creative juices going.

6. Look at cutting your expenses while you are in college. Go to an in-state college. If you can live at home, it will cut down more expenses. Consider taking CLEP exams. You

can study, take a test, and then get the college credit if you pass. Some colleges will put a limit on how many credits you can transfer in with CLEP classes. It's the fastest and the most affordable way to get college classes for those people who are self-motivated learners. My wife used this method to complete 75% of the coursework for her degree.

7. Consider joining the military. Jim went to medical school, which was fully paid for by the Air Force. He then served in the Air Force one year for each year that he went to school.

Thank you for sharing this journey with me to Biblical financial freedom. May the Lord bless you as you follow His path.

If you enjoyed this book, share it with a friend and leave a review on Amazon. Thank you for joining me in the journey.

Pastor Jonathan Geraci

Made in the USA
Middletown, DE
30 July 2018